BRET RIDGWAY

VIEW FROM THE BACK

101 Tips For Event Promoters Who Want To *Dramatically Increase Back-of-the-Room Sales*

NEW YORK

VIEW FROM THE BACK

101 Tips for Event Promoters Who Want to
Dramatically Increase Back-of-the-Room Sales
BRET RIDGWAY

ISBN: 1-60037-217-1 (Paperback)

ISBN: 1-60037-218-X (eBook)

Published by:

MORGAN · JAMES
THE ENTREPRENEURIAL PUBLISHER

Morgan James Publishing, LLC
1225 Franklin Ave Ste 325
Garden City, NY 11530-1693
Toll Free 800-485-4943
www.MorganJamesPublishing.com

Cover & Interior Design by:
Heather Kirk
www.BrandedForSuccess.com
Heather@BrandedForSuccess.com

Habitat for Humanity®
Peninsula
Building Partner

Experts Are Raving About *View From The Back*

"Believe me, the secrets Bret reveals in *View From The Back* will mean a difference in your bottom line. Most new promoters drastically underestimate all the things that can cost or make you money — therefore they fail. <u>Anybody</u> who is or who wants to do events should read this book. A beginner who doesn't read this book 10 times is asking for an expensive lesson. After all, at the end of the day — an event <u>can</u> make you a huge sum of money. Do it ALL right."

~Ted Ciuba, www.ThinkAndGrowRich.com

"After implementing just one tip — #31 — my back-of-the-room sales dollars increased 10%. Thanks, Bret!"

~Donna Fox, www.CreditMillionaire.com

"In the very competitive market of Seminar Marketing, it becomes critically important to use any little 'trick-of-the-trade' to put more people in seats and run an effective and profitable event. Bret Ridgway has created the greatest tips book in *View From The Back* for seminar promoters I've ever seen. In fact, nothing else even comes close to the powerful, actionable tips contained in this insightful publication.

"I've already found and begun using several of these tips to enhance the value of my own seminars and give my profits a quantum leap.

Bottom line: Bret's stuff works ... and I've already seen it add thousands in extra profits. My only regret is that my competitors may soon have this book. I pray my competitors never get their hands on it... it's just too good and dangerous in the wrong hands."

~Michael Penland, **Internet and Joint Venture Marketing Super Conference!,** *www.InstantCashMarketing.com*

"I first met Bret Ridgway at a table in the back of a room at an Internet marketing seminar in Las Vegas, Nevada. Now, my investment of less than $1000 in books, tapes and continuing education with Bret has since transformed to over 10,000 times that to increase and enhance my business and improve my family life.

"Bret Ridgway and what he's learned over the years as the de facto standard back-of-the-room table where he sells continuing education for speakers and other events is my single most important contact in the seminar business.

"Through his eyes I've met other speakers; through his contacts, I have made joint venture partnerships; and through his direction I will continue to grow my business because he sees what other people don't see.

"Learn from this man. Study what he teaches. And know that when you're sitting in the back of the room, you're leading from behind and get to see what's happening at the event behind closed doors."

~Alex Mandossian, www.AskMyList.com

Introduction & Acknowledgements

Way back in 1992, I had the fortunate privilege of attending *Gary Halbert's* "Hurricane Andrew Seminar" in Key West, Florida. Little did I know at the time how that event would change my life and the interesting paths that it would lead me down.

It's fascinating to me how one can track a line back from a specific event to another event to another event and know exactly how they got to where they're at today. This book is a direct result (or maybe I should say an indirect result) of that event that happened over a dozen years ago.

Of course, there were specific things that occurred that even led me to being in Key West those few years ago, but for the purposes of this story that's where it all began. *Gary Halbert's* seminar was my first exposure to the world of direct marketing outside of the world of telemarketing, which I had been involved with for about ten years.

But over the course of those few days back in 1992 I had the wonderful opportunity to learn from masters like *Gary Halbert, Ted Nicholas, Bill Myers, David Deutsch, Brad* and *Alan Antin* and many others. It's also where I had the opportunity to meet *Carl Galletti* for the first time.

That chance meeting led to a joint venture with Carl two or three years later where I took over Carl's hard-to-find marketing books catalog. You can still find this catalog online today at <u>SFSBookstore.com</u>.

Fast forward to 1999. Carl decided to put on his first Internet Marketing Superconference in Las Vegas and asked me if I would come out and set up a marketing bookstore at his event and handle the back-of-the-room sales. I had only a vague idea of what that entailed but it sounded like a great opportunity to learn and meet some new folks so I agreed to come out and help Carl.

That one event evolved into the eventual formation of Speaker Fulfillment Services (SpeakerFulfillmentServices.com) as we know it today. And it's still evolving. Some of the speakers at Carl's event, who were event promoters in their own right, saw what we were doing and asked us if we could help at their event.

As a result, we've had the opportunity to handle the back-of-the room sales table for several dozen events over the last six years. Some of the events were small, with only a couple dozen attendees, and others have had several hundred people in attendance. While many of the events have been in the Internet marketing arena, all of the event promoter's have relied upon back-of-the-room sales for a significant chunk of their profits from their conference, seminar, or bootcamp.

We've had a great window to view what promoter's can do to help stimulate their back-of-the-room sales. And also what some promoter's have done that has absolutely killed their event sales. Not intentionally, of course, but the effect was the same as if they'd built a moat around their sales table.

This book, *A View From The Back — 101 Tips for Event Promoters Who Want to Increase Their Back-of-the-Room Sales*, is a direct result of all the good, the bad, and the ugly I've seen over the last few years — both as an event attendee and as the guy in the back of the room. In no way do I proclaim to be the inventor of most of the tips you'll find in this book.

This introduction wouldn't be complete without acknowledging some of the people who have allowed us the privilege of handling the back of the room at their events — great marketers like *Carl Galletti, Armand Morin, Ted Ciuba, Randy Charach, Rhea Perry, Michael Penland, Fred Gleeck, Brett McFall, Tom Hua, Bob Silber* and *Willie Crawford*. I salute all of you who have the courage to take on the role of event promoter.

And to some of the speakers and others I've had the great fortune to meet at these conferences who I am now blessed to count many as both friends and colleagues — *Alex Mandossian, John Childers, Debra Thompson, Marianna Morin, Michel Fortin, Paul Colligan, Declan Dunn, John Assaraf, Stephen Pierce, Jim Edwards,* and *Mike Stewart* just to name a few. You all inspire me in ways you cannot imagine.

~Bret Ridgway, Speaker Fulfillment Services

Foreword

The seminar industry is a multi-billion dollar industry. Yes, I said Billion. Yes, it's profitable. Yes, it's rewarding. And yes, you can also lose the shirt on your back if you do not have the specific knowledge to carry out an event, workshop or seminar.

Having run some of the most successful seminars in my industry, I know the key to putting on and running a successful event is to surround yourself with people who absolutely know what they are doing and I have done just that with Bret Ridgway.

It was several years ago that I met Bret Ridgway.

Where you ask? At a seminar. He was working the back table at this event. I was pretty new to the seminar industry. In fact, this was one of the first seminars that I had went to. I knew there were back-of-the-room sales, I knew there were speakers who sold products.

What I didn't know was how all this was done, but I knew someone else must know.

Coincidentally or not, the next several events I went to, Bret was right there again working the back-of-the-room sales and management for the event promoter.

I had to ask myself, "Why does everyone seem to be using this one person?"

It's very simple, he knows what he is doing. Shortly after, I started what has turned into the largest Internet Marketing seminar in the world — the "BigSeminar." Who do you think I asked to run the back table for me? You guessed it, Bret Ridgway.

The greatest line pertaining to business in a movie is from Jerry Maguire. There was this one statement... "It's not showfriends... it's showbusiness". Interesting. I thought about this, long after I saw the movie. It's so true.

I see the mistakes many people make when attempting to do their first seminar or really any seminar for that matter. When you get there, it's like a family reunion for the promoter. My brother is running camera; my sister is taking orders; my best friend is managing the sales — you get the picture. I have no problem with this as long as they are qualified. Business is about turning a profit. It sounds hard and cold, but it's true.

Do you really want to put your and your family's livelihood on the line because you don't want to hurt you brother's feelings?

I run several multi-million dollar companies. I look for three qualities in every person who I bring into my inner circle:

1. Do I trust them.

2. Are they loyal?

3. Do they follow through?

This book you are holding in your hands is from a person who has met all three of those qualities with me and I can assure you, this information presented is information you can take to the bank.

People have a misconception that "tips" aren't worth anything. Let me put it into perspective for you. If you were given a small tip to buy Microsoft stock in 1988 what would that have been worth? The tips you have in your hands are worth just as much.

Take them and implement them into your event, workshop or seminar and you too will be running the most successful events and seminars in your industry.

~Armand Morin, BigSeminar.com, GeneratorSoftware.com

Table of Contents

TIP #1
Continuing Education

Make it known early in your event that your speakers will be offering "continuing education" regarding the topic on which they are speaking. While you expect your speakers to deliver great content during their allotted time you know there is no way they can cover all the nitty gritty details on their area of expertise during the limited time they have.

Make it clear that all the continuing education offered is a choice. But if you teach "continuing education" from the beginning when you promote the event and during the event as emcee between the speakers than you'll get more sales.

TIP #2
Stimulate Buying Behavior Early

You **want to get your** attendees comfortable with going to your order table early in an event. So offer a low-cost product sometime the first morning of the conference that requires the participants to go to the order table to purchase.

You're stimulating buying behavior and breaking down that initial resistance to handing money over.

It doesn't even have to be the attendee's own money. A technique I've seen used with great success at an event is to first affix a dollar bill to the bottom of the chair of each person. Then offer a book for a dollar which can be claimed by turning in the dollar bill which they'll find fastened to their chair. Almost every one of your dollars will come back to you and your participants will know quickly how to get to the order table and hand over money.

TIP #3
Merchant Account Classification

When you set up your account initially make sure the provider understands exactly what type of sales you'll be running through your account. Your account needs to be classified so that event sales are an accepted transaction type.

I've had more than one speaker call me after an event and tell me they couldn't process the sales from an event they did because their merchant provider says their account is not rated for that type of sale.

Nothing is more embarrassing than having monies "frozen" by your merchant provider because you didn't set up your account properly in the first place. You probably need those funds to pay all your speakers and other vendors, so don't get yourself in trouble by not having the right type of merchant account before you begin.

Tell your merchant account provider that you are in the education business. First — so they won't have a problem with the sale of products. Second, don't say the "seminar business." This is considered a red flag to merchant providers and may make them more wary of your business and wanting to questions all or some of your future transactions.

TIP #4
Merchant Account Awareness

If you do events on an irregular schedule then your merchant account provider will witness wide swings in the amount of money processed from your company. For weeks there may be low or no activity and then you might run several hundred thousand dollars through your account in a three day period.

The key here is communication. Alert your provider ahead of time as to what your event schedule is and what volume level they might anticipate seeing at specific times. I've found that if you keep the channels of communication open with your merchant account provider and don't hit them with "surprises" then things go a lot more smoothly.

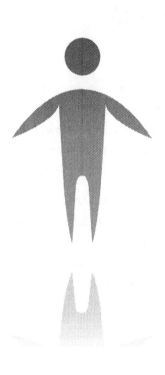

TIP #5
Platform Selling Skills

Are your speakers trained to sell from the platform? I've heard dozens of presentations where a speaker delivered great content, had continuing education to offer, but was clueless on how to deliver an effective sales close from the stage.

You might want to consider only including speakers on your platform who have a track history of generating significant back-of-the-room sales. The pros will have gone through some type of continuing education themselves on platform selling skills.

If you have a speaker who you really want to have as part of your program, but who hasn't sold before, you might want to suggest they do some type of formal speaker training that will help with their platform selling skills.

The following people offer speaker training programs:

→   John Childers — JohnChilders.com

→   Les Brown — LesSpeaks.com

→   T. Harv Eker — PeakPotentials.com

Be sure to examine their content carefully in order to select the training course that would be the best fit for you.

Whenever you're considering a speaker for your stage see if you can talk with other event promoters who have used that speaker before. How well did they sell? Did their sales stick or did they have a high rate of returns? How was their follow-up with customers after the event?

TIP #6
What Did I Buy Again?

I've seen it time and time again. A speaker delivers a fantastic presentation and people are flocking to your sales table to order the speakers product or service. But they're not quite sure what they're ordering but they know the offer sounded too good to pass up.

So what do you usually have from your speaker? If you're lucky you have an order form that lists what people will receive for signing up for their offer. But you may have only a fill in the blanks order form with no offer details whatsoever.

Insist your speakers develop an "Offer Summary Sheet" that details exactly what people will receive when they sign up. This can be handed to people when they order or to those that need clarification on the offer prior to ordering. I've witnessed a lot of lost sales because the participants didn't clearly understand the offer made from the stage.

TIP #7
Dedication Is A Key

Use a dedicated sales staff for your order table at your event rather than having a speaker collect their own orders. It's not that you don't trust your speakers — you should if you've asked them to speak on your platform. It's so that your attendees always know where to go to order their continuing education.

I know some event promoters who simply put their speakers on the honor system to process their own orders and pay the promoter the money due them. Others want to have more intimate knowledge of how well each speaker has done so they have all the monies run through their order table. You'll have to decide which model is right for you.

I feel a consistent ordering process is critical to your back-of-the-room sales and would encourage you to follow this model.

TIP #8
Go Totally Triplicate

Whether you're providing order forms for everyone or you're having your speakers provide their own order forms, try and go with a triplicate form or what is known as an NCR form and can easily be done at FedEx-Kinkos. That way there is a copy for the customer to take with them, a copy for the speaker, and a copy for you.

You should have your order table folks staple a copy of the "Order Summary Sheet" as described in Tip #6 to the customer's copy of the order form. Especially if the speaker's order form doesn't include a detailed list of what is included in their show special.

Your customers need a copy of their order form. They've likely just spent several hundred or thousands of dollars and need a record of what they bought. It helps the sales stick and it provides professional customer service to the individual. It also saves you time as a promoter from having to fax a copy of the receipt to the customer later.

TIP #9
Buying Units

When you're projecting the amount in back-of-the-room sales you're going to have at your event, it's critical to know the number of buying units you have in your room. This can vary from speaker to speaker because the size of your crowd will change during the course of your event. In an ideal world every attendee stays in the room and listens to every presenter, but get used to the fact that this will probably never happen.

A buying unit does not mean the number of people in the room. A man who attends a conference and brings his wife along as his guest would be only one buying unit even though it's two people. An entrepreneur and his office manager would typically represent only one buying unit. So you need to understand who is "attached" to who in your crowd so you can have a good idea of how many buying units you have in your room at any given time.

When you're evaluating how well a speaker sold you must take into account the number of buying units that were in the room during his or her presentation. Your after lunch speaker that sells $50K that is missing half of your crowd because they're late getting back from lunch is probably of more value to you than the person that sells $70K and has the entire crowd to speak to. At the least, your $50K person may deserve a better time slot at your next event.

TIP #10
Cell Phones No-Nos

Your speaker has just made a great presentation and is just beginning to work your audience into a buying frenzy. You can see they're starting to chomp at the bit to run to the back table and order their event package.

Then, ring-ring-ring, someone's cell phone goes off in the audience. It's simply the cutest little ring tone they just downloaded last week. Your speaker is distracted and loses their train of thought. The momentum for the sale is lost and you can just sense the energy seeping out of your crowd.

Ever happen? You bet it has. A professional speaker won't let something like a cell phone derail them, but that doesn't mean your audience's attention hasn't been knocked off the tracks.

That's why it's so important to remind your attendees at the beginning of each day and after a long lunch break to turn their phones off or at least put them on vibrate. You're not going to get them to leave their cell phones in their hotel room, but you can minimize the possibilities of distractions with a pleasant little reminder at appropriate times during your event. Part of your welcome packets or your daily agenda should include a cell phone reminder.

TIP #11
Do Deferred Payments Pay Off?

When your event will feature several speakers who will each be offering a high priced package you may want to consider having some of your speakers offer some type of deferred payment plan to increase the number of sign ups for their offer.

At a multiple day event if you've had any back-of-the-room success at all your attendees may be a little money weary if they've already invested in one or more continuing education products from some of the speakers. So the ability for them to spread out their payments over a few month period will make the offer more attractive.

The bookkeeping for deferred payments can be a bit of a hassle and your speakers will need to understand that some of their money will be deferred because you haven't collected all the money yet, but the increased sales that can result may justify offering terms of some type to the attendees.

TIP #12
Delivered or Not Delivered?

Sometimes your event has speakers who bring their product to the event to be delivered and others who don't bring any product. And then some of the speakers who have brought product only bring a handful of sets, so some of their orders can be fulfilled on site and others can't.

It can become very confusing after the event to keep track of what's been delivered or not delivered unless you have clear instructions on each individual order as to what needs to happen post event.

We've gone to utilizing a self-inking red stamp that reads "Delivered" to highlight orders that were fulfilled at the event. This way there is no question when you're preparing a summary of orders for a speaker as to whether a certain customer has received their product or not.

We're using a similar red stamp to highlight anything on an order that is outside the "norm". We consider the "norm" to be credit card payment in full at the event with all products to be shipped after the event. Some of the stamps you could use include:

→ Deferred Payments

→ Paid by Cash

→ Paid by Check # _____

→ Partial Delivery

→ Delayed Shipment

→ See Special Notes Below

The key is to develop a system and then train your sales staff to follow the system and be consistent.

TIP #13
Rewarding Speakers Who Fill The Seats

Here's something new I've heard recently discussed but haven't had the opportunity to witness in person yet. That is rewarding your speakers who helped put people in the seats at your event with a higher percentage of their own sales at the event.

The normal promoter/speaker split of sales at an event is 50/50. On a $1000 dollar sale the speakers gets $500 and the promoter gets $500. Credit card fees are covered by the promoter out of their 50% and product duplication costs are covered by the speaker out of their 50%.

But what if you offered incentives to your speakers to really promote the event hard by offering them 55% — 60% or more of their own sales at the event if they sold more seats? It's usually very challenging to get your speakers to promote your event. I think this is an idea worth testing to see if it has a positive impact.

TIP #14
Avoid Content Overlap

When lining up the speakers for your event you should have a curriculum approach in mind. Each speaker's content can build upon the previous speakers or fill in the missing pieces from earlier presentations.

What you should probably NOT do is simply pick your speakers by name only with each speaker having carte blanche to speak about whatever topic they choose. What you invariably end up with is more than one speaker talking about the same topic.

Not only do your attendees feel cheated because they've "heard it before" but the second or third speaker who speaks about the same subject will suffer dramatically at the sales table. Which means you suffer also.

TIP #15
Speakers On Parade

A **technique I've seen used** quite frequently at events that seems to work very well is to have those speakers who are already at the event get introduced to the audience on the first morning. Each gives a five minute intro on what topic they'll be speaking about and when they'll be presenting.

The benefits are two fold. First, it begins to build the comfort level your attendees have with the individual speakers. So when the speaker begins their regularly scheduled presentation the audience is already familiar with them and the first level of trust has already been established.

Secondly, it builds in your audience an anticipation of things to come. Your goal is to make sure you keep as many as possible of the attendees in their seats for all the speakers. When the students get to hear directly from the speaker what his topic is going to be, and that topic really resonates with them, then you can be sure they'll make it back into the room at the right time.

TIP #16
Those Rowdy Speakers

Let's face it — conferences are typically the only time your speakers see each other. So it's kind of like old home week. There's a lot of story telling, idea swapping, and general B.S.-ing. The only problem is that sometimes they want to do it in your meeting room while another speaker is presenting!

I'm not implying that the speakers are ever doing anything to intentionally distract from another speaker. They just sometimes, well, get carried away.

Don't hesitate to ask your rowdy bunch to take their discussion out of the meeting room if they are causing too much of a ruckus. A friendly reminder to them that they wouldn't want someone else talking over their presentation is all it takes.

TIP #17
Networking Negatives?

One of the biggest draws for many events is the networking opportunities it will provide for its attendees. If your event is to be successful long term you'll want the same. Friendships are strengthened and deals are made in the hallways outside your meeting room throughout the day.

Therein lays the Catch-22. If they're making deals out in the hallway then they're not in their seats listening to the current speaker. You'll need to recognize that this isn't necessarily a negative thing. Yes, you might lose a few ears from the room. But the buzz you're hoping to create for your event as a "can't miss" spot to be is usually worth the tradeoff.

You'll also want to specifically arrange special networking activities — a reception the night before, lunch with the speakers, etc. to get more positive vibes for your event. And make sure those people that want to talk during a presentation are far enough away from the door to your meeting room that they're not bothering anyone in the room trying to listen to your speaker.

TIP #18
Breaking Away From Breaks

As I've heard many times before in some form or other, "The mind can only comprehend what the butt can endure." Bottom line — you'll need breaks. Your challenge is always how to get the people back into your room in a timely manner so they're ready to hear the next presenter.

First, you need a person who has the specific responsibility of herding people back into the room for each session. Obviously, you want them to do this in as nice of a manner as possible because you don't want to upset anyone.

Do NOT have this person be the same person who is in charge of the sales table. You never want to interrupt someone at the sales table from closing a sale.

Whether you use a ting-a-ling bell, flashing strobe lights, an a-ooga horn, or some other way to let the crowd know it's time to head back into the meeting room it doesn't really matter. Just train them early in the event what the get ready to go signal is and you'll have a lot more success breaking away from your breaks.

TIP #19
Overwhelming Offers

Make sure your speakers apply the KISS principle to their offers at your event. KISS, of course, means "keep it simple stupid". I've seen speakers offer as many as five separate deals to the audience and by the time they got through explaining each part of each offer and the pricing the audience was so confused they bought nothing. And I've seen this done by well-known, big-name marketers.

Tell your speakers to make one offer only. It's take it or leave it. Some speakers will rebel and want to make two offers. That's okay — what you want to absolutely prevent are the complicated, multi-faceted offers that take thirty minutes to explain and over-whelm your audience like a tidal wave.

John Childers' says "A confused mind says NO!" Heed these words well and make sure your speakers keep their offers simple.

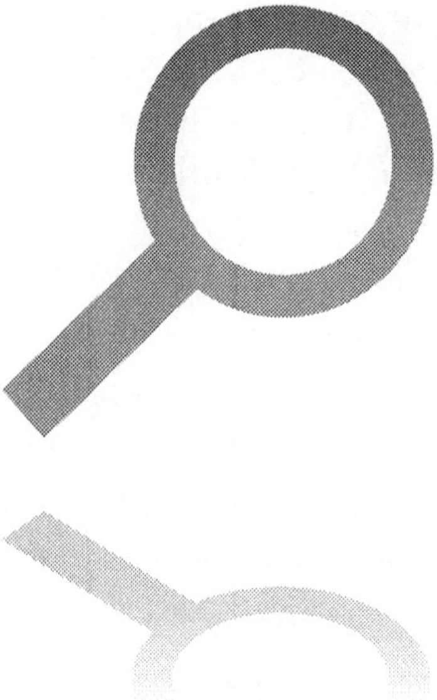

TIP #20
Meditate to Mediocrity

Here's a sales killer I've seen first hand. Your well-intentioned emcee grabs the microphone immediately after a speaker has finished his close. He begins, *"Close your eyes and picture this. Imagine yourself on a tropical island and..."*

Your speaker has just busted his gut delivering a fantastic presentation and a great close on his continuing education opportunity, and your emcee is trying to send your crowd into a state of meditation when they should be headed back to your sales table.

I call this "Meditate to Mediocrity." This is because mediocre is what your speaker's back-of-the-room sales will be if you allow your emcee to practice this tactic. I'm not saying there isn't an appropriate time for meditation — it's just not after a speaker has delivered his close.

To prevent this, have each speaker close himself/herself out. Have them instruct your audience what to do next.

TIP #21
Should You Allow Q&A?

There's nothing wrong with allowing a speaker to have a question and answer period as part of their presentation. In fact, speaker panels where the audience can ask any one of a number of speakers a question is usually one of the most highly valued portions of an event.

First, you want to make sure the individual speaker is adept at handling questions from the audience. A more experienced speaker can typically handle it pretty well. But a newer speaker can get so bogged down in questions they never get around to delivering all of the content they had initially promised. So I would generally steer away from allowing your newer platform speakers to do Q & A sessions.

Secondly, if the speaker takes questions and answers at the end of their presentation they can kill any opportunity to sell their continuing education opportunity. Make sure you clearly communicate with a speaker that intends to do Q & A that they need to wrap up their question period before their sales presentation so they can do justice to selling their back-of-the-room product or service.

TIP #22
Real-Time Processing

If you're going to process your orders at the event I encourage you to do it in real time. The discount rate your merchant account provider gives you is typically half of a percent or greater less if a card is "swiped" rather than keyed in. The merchant account provider considers a swiped card a more secure transaction and rewards you accordingly.

That means you'll need either wireless terminals or a terminal hooked to a phone line to be able to process the credit cards in real time. Hotels typically charge between $100 to $200 or more to provide a phone line. And they may also hit you with a small charge for each outgoing call even if it's to a toll-free number.

Is it worth it? On average it costs us about $200 to have a live phone line at the sales table to hook a credit card terminal to. But, if you're doing just $100,000 in back-of-the-room sales then you're savings, due to the lower discount rate, is at least .005 x 100,000 or $500. So you put a few hundred dollars more in your pocket and were able to provide your purchasers with a signed receipt right on the spot.

If you plan to use wireless terminals always make sure they will function properly in the exact location where they will be used. We've tested terminals on one side of a lobby in a hotel and they worked fine. But when the event began the sales table was set up on an opposite wall and we were unable to pick up a satisfactory signal.

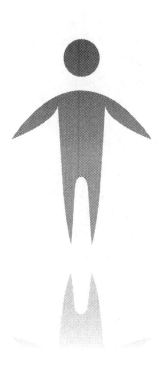

TIP #23
How Many Order Takers And Terminals Do I Need?

You need to make sure you have enough terminals to handle the size of your crowd. An event with 100 or less people can usually be handled quite easily with a single terminal and a couple order takers. If your crowd is larger, than consider bring two to three terminals and at least four people to work your order table.

If we're asked to do an event, then I usually provide one person per 50 attendees to work the back-of-the-room sales table. And one terminal for every two people usually works fine. There is no harm in having more bodies available if the space at your sales table permits it and the cost of those additional people isn't excessive.

You can usually find volunteers willing to work for free just to have the chance to hang out at the event and meet people. Just be sure they understand their first priority is providing you assistance at the sales table.

TIP #24
How Much Time Is Enough?

How much time should you allot your speakers on stage? I've been to events where speakers have had as few as 15 minutes to as much as 3 hours of speaking time. So how much time is not enough and how much is too much?

The answer is, of course, it depends. The easy side of the equation is the minimum amount of time you should give your speaker. And that's 90 minutes. I've found that an hour or less of speaking time causes a speaker to rush through his content to get to his sales pitch. If you stack up a lot of speakers back to back with one hour speaking windows then your event will probably get classified as a "pitch fest".

However, 90 minutes allows your speaker ample time to deliver good solid content for at least 75 minutes before offering their continuing education opportunity. If a speaker has completed their presentation quicker than that then it's okay to go short of the full 90 minutes. I'd rather give my attendees a slightly longer break than have a speaker ramble on just to fill up the allotted time.

But how much time is too much? Here's where the "it depends" really comes in to play. If your speaker has great rapport with your audience and they're hanging on every word then two to three hours may well be okay. You might need a butt break part way through but that's okay.

But if your speaker is a real snoozer than two to three minutes might be too long. Not that we ever have speakers who don't meet our expectations.

Keep in mind that you need to strike a balance between the number of selling opportunities at your event (read, more speakers) and the amount of content you deliver (read, less speakers) — 90 to 120 minutes seems to be an optimal time range.

TIP #25
Rapid Refunds

I **have yet to go to an event** where someone who has purchased a continuing education package hasn't had buyer's remorse and asked for a refund a week or two after the event. Just accept it as a part of doing business.

Issue the refund right away in whatever format your customer wants. If they don't have a preference then tell them you'll issue a refund check. That way your merchant account doesn't have as many negative "hits" on it then it would if you were strictly refunding credit cards.

You'll need to remember to notify the speaker of the return so that if there is any product that hasn't been shipped yet it doesn't get shipped. **If product was delivered at the event to the customer then you'll want to require the return of any physical products in good condition prior to issuing the refund.**

You should always clearly state what your refund policy for purchases made at the event is. It is common these days for promoters to offer a 30 day refund policy and if the speaker wants to extend that refund period than any refunds issued after that 30 days is complete are entirely out of the speaker's pocket.

TIP #26
Lead Them And They Will Follow

After a speaker has concluded his/her presentation have one of your event assistants lead the speaker directly back to the order table to field additional questions and help close the sales. No one knows the product better than the speaker and you will have questions about their package that the crew at the sales table probably can't answer. Better answers mean more sales.

Moving the speaker back to your sales table also allows your audio crew and set up people to get things properly prepared for the next speaker on your schedule. If you have a crowd of people around the stage you'll find it very difficult to get ready for the next presentation.

TIP #27
Order Table Hours

How long each day should you plan on having your order table up and ready to go? On the first day things should be set up at least half an hour before the kick off of the event ONLY if you're running a bookstore and selling non-speaker products that people may want to browse through. If you're selling no other products then what the speaker himself offers than just have things ready to go by the time things get started.

On subsequent days I recommend having your order table set up and ready to roll at least 30 minutes before the first speaker of the day. If you're running a "bookstore" you'll need to be prepared for your browsers again. And you may have some folks who want to order something offered the previous day but they were too tired at the end of the previous day to get it done.

At the conclusion of each day of your event I recommend keeping your sales table open for a minimum of 30 minutes and sometimes up to an hour after the last speaker has finished. People will continue to mill about the meeting room and talk for some time after speakers have finished for the day.

On the last day of the event remain open for at least an hour after conclusion. You'll have some attendees who have been pondering the various continuing education offers throughout the weekend and they won't make their choice until after the last speaker has finished. If you close your table up right away you may lose some serious money. I've seen tens of thousands of dollars worth of products and services purchased over an hour after the event has officially ended.

TIP #28
Handling Disruptive Influences

Hopefully, **this won't happen** to you at an event, but chances are, it will sometime. You'll have a person in the crowd who isn't getting what they expected out of the event. So they start complaining loudly during breaks or even while a speaker is still presenting.

The best advice — get rid of them right away. One bad apple can quickly ruin the whole bunch in this scenario. Politely pull them away from your other attendees and tell them something like, "Mr. Jones, I'm sorry, but it's obvious you aren't getting from this event what you expected. I'm going to write you a check right now for the amount of your registration and I'm sorry this didn't work out for you."

Do not allow them to poison your crowd in any way. You'll lose a lot more in back-of-the-room sales due to the negative vibes from your complainer than you will in refunding the registration fees and removing the toxin from your room.

TIP #29
Selling On Scarcity

Sometimes a speaker will make an offer that has limited availability. Perhaps it's seats to an event where there is truly limited seating, or it's consulting time and they only have so many hours in the day they can make available for that type of activity. Maybe they just brought along a limited amount of physical product with them so the scarcity lies in the number of people that will be able to take the product with them from the event.

First, the sales table will need to know whether the limited number offered is a hard and fast number, or just a sales tactic to trigger more purchases. Yes, it does happen.

If it's a true limited opportunity, then your sales staff will need to number the order forms as they come in to keep track of who is really entitled to receive the special offer. Sometimes additional bonuses are offered to the first "x" people who sign up. So you'll need to keep careful track of the signups to avoid confusion and possible disappointment.

TIP #30
Let's Get Physical

If part of a speaker's special offer includes a physical product — books, manuals, CDs, DVDs, etc., then be sure that they provide an actual sample for display on the sales table. People like to see what they're buying or browse through what they're considering buying. If they know it's "real" then they're more comfortable making the purchase.

The speaker can either provide a mockup of their product or a complete finished set the first buyer can take with them at the conclusion of the event. Having a physical product at the event also allows the speaker to display it from the front of the room during their sales pitch.

It's also good to have a physical product to review with your sales team so they can be better prepared to represent the speaker and close the sale.

If the speaker chooses to display the product in the front of the room during their presentation make sure you have someone to set up the product before they present and someone to bring the product back to the sales table for display during the break after they present. You don't want to have the speaker responsible for this. Nor do you want someone from the sales table to leave the table during the middle of a sales rush to bring product back.

TIP #31
Upselling To More Sales

We do it all the time online. And, if you've ever ordered from an infomercial, you've undoubtedly experienced it. What is it? It's upselling. At the key ordering point, you're asked if you want to add something else to your order for a special price.

How come we rarely see it done at the back of the room? You should. Just get your speakers to come up with a special upsell offer that they don't even mention on the stage. But when the customer's are ordering their event package your back-of-the-room staff asks if they'd like to take advantage of the special additional offer. Enough people will take advantage of it to make it well worth your while.

TIP #32
Event Audios And Videos

I **see this quite frequently,** and it really bugs me because I know the promoter is leaving a lot of money on the table when they do this. They're recording their event and planning to offer the event audios and videos to people after the event.

Yet, they don't offer the people attending the event the opportunity to order the audios and/or videos for a special price at the event itself. Event recordings typically sell for a few hundred dollars, so even if only a small percentage of your audience wishes to invest in the discs for after event review purposes it can amount to several thousands of dollars in sales.

Plus, it's your product so you don't have to split the revenues 50/50 with a speaker. If you're going to record your event always, always offer the discs to the event attendees.

I would not offer the event audios or videos to the attendees until the very end of the event — after all the individual speakers have closed their sales.

TIP #33
Audience Demographics

Almost any professional speaker will want to know the demographics of the audience they'll be speaking to before the event. This allows them to tailor their presentation to better address the background and needs of your audience.

What are some of the demographics your speakers might want to know?

→ Experience level of the attendees

→ Male or female

→ Age

→ Did they fly in or are they commuting to the event

→ Have they attended one of your events previously

→ What was the cost to attend the event

→ What percentage of the crowd are paid attendees

Any information of this type that you can provide your speakers ahead of time will help them to prepare a better presentation for your audience. The better the presentation, the better the rapport between your speakers and your attendees, the more in back-of-the-room sales you'll generate.

TIP #34
Speaker Separation

How long a break should you take between speakers? If your speaker is selling from the platform you need to allow a minimum of 15 minutes between the end of his presentation and the beginning of the next speaker. I'm seeing more and more events go to a 30 minute break between each speaker. If your schedule will accommodate it, I would lean more toward the 30 minute separation rather than the 15.

The longer break time allows your first presenter time to finish answering questions about their package at the sales table and get those sales wrapped up before the next speaker. Your attendees appreciate the longer time because they don't have to rush to the bathroom and will still have time to do additional networking at your event.

The longer break also gives your students some absorption time. The talk of the first speaker can sink in a little bit before they are gearing up right away for another speaker.

Another consideration is the size of your audience. For crowds around 50 people, 15 minutes will usually work fine. For crowds around 100, consider at least 20 minutes as a minimum, and for crowds over 100, allow 30 minutes — and no more.

Make sure you have enough sales staff on hand to handle the sales and make sure your attendees can get in and out of the facilities in time between speakers.

TIP #35
Mastering Music

It's critical for your event's success to keep the enthusiasm of your crowd high throughout the event. Use appropriate music to pump the crowd up as a new speaker takes the stage and as they exit the stage to head to the sales table at the conclusion of their presentation.

Do NOT keep the music blaring so loud during the breaks that the people in the room can't even carry on a conversation without yelling. You'll kill some of your best networking opportunities.

Make sure you're using royalty free music for your intros and exits to avoid any of the legal issues associated with playing music in a public venue.

TIP #36
Those Darn Doors

Even minor disruptions can ruin the flow of a speaker and negatively impact your back-of-the-room sales. Take for instance something as seemingly minor as the doors into your meeting room.

First, you want to be sure that the entry into your meeting room is always from the back of the room. That way those people that walk in after a speaker has already begun his presentation aren't distracting the folks already in the room. All eyes naturally turn to someone coming into their field of vision so remove this distraction by making entry available only at the back. Fire codes won't allow you to lock the front doors, but a sign stating "Use Other Doors ——>" will do the trick.

A second common problem with doors is they clang when they are opened and closed. This minor disruption can be handled by taping the latch open so it doesn't latch properly or by hanging a towel over the top edge of the door so that it doesn't close completely. Just be sure you're not keeping it so open that outside noises are interrupting your room.

TIP #37
Immediate Deliverables

When your speakers offer a large package from the stage it can typically include downloadable information, future coaching sessions, or physical products which are not going to be delivered on site.

An important "stick strategy" you should employ to make sure the sales made at your event stay sold is to have the speaker provide some part of their package that can be delivered to the customer at the point of sale. It can be a CD, DVD, or manual. It can be part of the regular package or a bonus item they receive for ordering at the event.

The key thing is to just give them something tangible that they can take with them from the event. Make sure on the sell sheet that you attach to their receipt that you clearly mark off any parts of the package they have received at the event.

TIP #38
Post-Event Speaker Communication

If you're processing the orders for all of your speakers then they're going to need the order information from you as quickly as possible in order to be able to fulfill the orders right away. If the speakers followed your recommendation of doing triplicate order forms then you can give them the hard copy of each order at the conclusion of the event.

If they didn't use a triplicate order form or left prior to the conclusion of the event then you'll need to email or fax them copies of the orders so they can do their fulfillment right away. We like to create an order summary for each speaker that we email to them within a couple days of the event that lists each individual order and totals up all their sales for the event. That way they know how much they should be expecting to be paid after the event.

TIP #39
Thump Value

My colleague, **Armand Morin,** calls this the "Holy Crap" factor. What it means is that with a physical product you want to be sure the perceived value is very high by having a lot of "stuff" in your package. The first words out of your customers mouth should be something like, "Holy crap, I get all this stuff as part of the package. That's great."

If one of your speakers wants to display his product on the order table and let's say he's selling a $1997.00 package. If the display consists of a couple CDs in jewel cases and a few stapled pages of printed materials then you don't have any "thump value" and product sales will suffer as a result.

So, if you're counting on the impressiveness of a product display to help sell a product package make sure the "thump value" is there.

TIP #40
Unlocking The Wallet

As a general rule, your attendees are not going to be ready to open up their wallet or purse the first morning of your event. Accordingly, the sales from your first speaker will be lower then they might normally be in a different time slot.

That's why it is important to have a pretty dynamic speaker early in your event to help get your crowd loosened up and beginning to spend some money. Most speakers don't consider this a prime speaking slot so you may have to "bribe" your kick off speaker with an additional slot later in the event.

But a good speaker is important for you to begin helping folks unlock their wallet or purse and begin spending money.

TIP #41
Pinching Pennies On Printing

In a word — **Don't!** Always have at least 10% more order forms available then the size of the crowd. People will invariably lose their form and when they want to order a product if you don't have a copy of the speaker's order form available then a sale might be lost.

I've literally seen $2000 sales lost because the customer "gave up" while waiting for someone to track down an order form for a certain speaker. Tell your speakers always to be over prepared rather than trying to save a couple dollars by not printing up a few more order forms.

As a back-up, you should always have a generic "event" order form that can be used for any speaker's offer in a pinch. You should have somewhere between five and seven times the number of generic order forms as the size of your crowd.

TIP #42
Speaker Accessibility

Encourage your speakers to attend your entire event, if possible. We routinely see the speaker who takes the time to get to know the attendees better by being accessible throughout the event is the speaker that has the highest back-of-the-room sales at the event.

If you have luncheons or dinners for your attendees the speakers will be joining, try and separate your speakers amongst the different tables. Don't let them all sit together like an "old boys" club that seems unapproachable to your regular attendees.

The more opportunities your participants have to interact with the speakers then the more each of those speakers that make themselves accessible will usually sell.

TIP #43
Let Your Sales Staff In On The Offer

Sometimes, it's impossible for a speaker to decide in advance exactly what his offer to your audience is going to be. Maybe he just hasn't thought it out yet or maybe he's waiting to see what kind of offer some of the other speakers make and how the audience has responded before finalizing his offer.

And we all know how it's common for a speaker to print a regular price on their order form and then have the audience mark out that price and write in a new price on the form.

You've got to make sure whatever the final offer is going to be is communicated to the entire sales staff prior to the speaker's close. Nothing looks worse then having an attendee come out to order a continuing education package and your sales staff having no clue what offer the speaker finally decided to make.

So you make sure the communication is in place to get the necessary information to your sales staff.

As a promoter you should always know what the amount of the speaker's offer is and you shouldn't have any surprises. If you don't get this information from the speaker then you should pull them off your platform. This is your event and you have an obligation to your audience to provide them the right speakers, prices, and products.

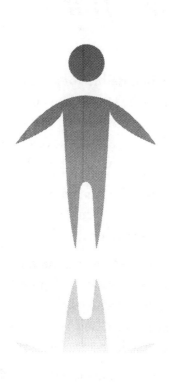

TIP #44
Speaker Staff Assistance

If a speaker wants to bring in a member of his or her staff to assist with the sales of their products by all means let them. In a fast-paced, multi-speaker event your sales staff will be deluged with different offers from all the speakers. Despite their best efforts they may become confused about what specific items are part of the speaker's continuing education package or what price point was finally decided upon.

A member of the speaker's staff should know that speaker's products inside out and can be a valuable addition to your sales staff to help answer questions on a temporary basis. This should result in more sales for your back-of-the-room operation.

So, let them in if a speaker wants to bring them along.

TIP #45
Hike Up Those Prices

I've witnessed a general evolution over the last five years at events to higher-priced packages from the speakers. In the earlier days, $47, $97, or $197 packages were pretty normal from the speakers, but folks are finally realizing that the effort required to sell a $47 package is pretty much the same as that required to sell a $1,997 package.

So, bigger bundles with higher price tags is more the norm these days. I'm talking $1,997, $2,997, $3,997, or higher. Certainly, a smaller number of people will order the package, but the revenues generated are usually far greater on a few sales at a higher price point then more sales at the lower price point.

It's common for newer speakers to undervalue their offering and price their products too low. Many promoters are communicating in advance with their speakers that the package they offer is expected to be above a certain dollar amount. Don't let your speakers go too low — it's taking money out of your pocket.

TIP #46
Harvesting Names

Going hand in hand with Tip #45 is the entire issue of harvesting names. You will have some speakers offer a give-away or try a very low priced option in order to try and "harvest" as many names from your audience as possible to add to their own database. Their thought is they'll make their money on the back end and the important thing is to get as many people as possible into their funnel at your event.

It's up to you to determine if you want to allow this type of name harvesting. Those promoters that communicate in advance with their speakers the minimum price points and no giveaways are trying to stop name harvesting. They know their money is in the back-of-the-room sales and not in what the speaker sells down the road to the attendees.

Other promoters are not concerned at all with the issue of name harvesting. Some speakers may even negotiate in advance that part of their "compensation" for speaking at the event will include the complete list of attendees. You'll have to decide if you want that speaker badly enough on your platform to "give" him the names you paid to get in the room.

The normal position of the event promoters is that it's their data-base and they've worked too hard to get the people in the room to allow any name harvesting. If a speaker does it and the promoter becomes aware the forms will be confiscated and it's highly unlikely the speaker will be invited to speak on that stage again.

TIP #47
Conference Cash

Mark Victor Hansen calls his "Mega Money". What is it? It's a coupon or certificate for $50 or $100 or whatever amount you decide that can be applied to the purchase of any speaker's back-of-the-room product or service.

It is awarded to people who sign up for your event as one of the perks for enrolling. Maybe you even want to award more "Conference Cash" to early enrollees. What a great way to help stimulate your back-of-the-room sales!

Of course, you'll want to limit the amount of conference cash an individual attendee can redeem. But, since its like "cash" at your event the attendees feel highly motivated to spend it so they don't lose it.

TIP #48
Pay Your Presenters Promptly

How soon after your event** should you pay your speakers? Of course, you need to allow time for the credit card payments you processed to be funded, and you want to make sure any checks you received for payment clear. You'll also want to allow some time for any sales that are completed after the close of the event to be properly handled.

Our rule of thumb is to pay speakers two weeks post event. Even then, you'll probably end up with some returns that will have to be refunded after that two-week period, which means your speaker will owe you money back if they've already been paid.

I even know some promoters who insist on 25% of the money due their speakers held in reserve to fund any returns made after that two-week period. Then, anywhere between 30 and 90 days after the event, if there haven't been any refunds, the remainder of the speaker's monies are paid.

Bottom line is you need to keep your speakers happy. So don't unnecessarily hold up their monies.

TIP #49
Special Deals

At some events, you'll have an attendee who has purchased some of a speaker's materials previously. So, they'll want a special deal to pick up the speaker's event package because they already have some of their stuff. It is always the speaker's discretion if he wants to allow a special deal other than what is printed on his order form.

The key is that the special deal be communicated clearly to the person who will process the order and that the order form be noted with a specific explanation of what deal was made. After the event it's difficult to remember details like this unless documentation exists.

The speaker should notify the sales table quietly that a special deal has been made for a particular attendee. You don't want to have bunches of people requesting special deals because they heard someone else received one.

TIP #50
Extra Sales Pitches

Should you allow a speaker extra time near the end of your event to present their offer again? They'll claim that several people have asked for more details, and it would be easiest to present before the entire group again.

From my experience, these extra sales pitches do not result in additional sales. First, it makes the speaker seem desperate, and it seems too pitchy. Second, they're stealing time from someone to have another closing opportunity.

It'll be your call as to whether you want to allow an additional "pitch." My experience shows it doesn't pay.

TIP #51
An Argumentative Speaker

I **wouldn't have believed it if** I hadn't seen it myself. A speaker had just completed his presentation and was promoting his event offer. He essentially told the audience they were stupid if they didn't buy into his $20K package.

Well, how did the audience react to being called "stupid?" As one might expect they weren't very happy. Some of the crowd began to argue with the speaker — who argued right back.

It got pretty ugly. No, fisticuffs didn't make an appearance, but you can imagine what the sales for that speaker ended up at. Zero, zip, nada. It's been several years since that fiasco, and I've yet to see that speaker back on the stage, which is a shame because he really does have some good content.

What should you do if this happens at your event? In as nice of a manner as possible, but as quickly as possible, yank this speaker from the stage. Anyone who alienates your audience will cause negative repercussions on the sales of upcoming speakers also. Unfortunately, this is a "cut your losses" scenario.

TIP #52
Keepin' It Cool

"It's freezing in here."

"It's too hot in here."

It seems to be one of the biggest complaints of every event — room temperature. You want your room to be comfortable, but the inflow and outflow of people seems to have your room temperature going up and down like a yo-yo.

I have yet to experience a meeting room that didn't fluctuate some, but you should aim for the cooler side rather than the warmer side. Advise your attendees to bring a sweater or jacket to put on if it gets too cool for them. If you keep it cool, people tend to be more alert (even if it's just from the shivering). :>)

If you go for warmer, you'll find your people ready to nod off, especially after lunch, and a snoozing audience isn't generally a buying audience.

TIP #53
PowerPoint-less

Make sure your speaker's have checked out their PowerPoint presentations on your system before it's presented. It's pointless to have a speaker stumbling around on stage because they can't get their PowerPoint presentation to work properly.

Even if they've done it at another event or they've tested it on their own system, have them do a check. A presentation that doesn't flow smoothly due to PowerPoint issues can be a real sales killer.

TIP #54
Audio Atrocities

In the same vein as Tip #53, be sure to test your audio systems fully before your event. Have plenty of back-up microphones and batteries and any other components that might fail and cause you to have audio difficulties.

Any "technical" aspect of your event needs to be tested and you need to have a back-up plan in the event of failure. What if the house lights go out mid-afternoon on your first day. You better have a back-up plan to keep your show going.

Maximization of your back-of-the-room sales comes from providing your attendees with a smooth flowing and fully integrated experience. Any blips can throw things off, so be prepared for almost any contingency.

TIP #55
Speaker Contact Information

Make sure that when an attendee orders a speaker's product at the sales table, they receive the contact information of the speaker at the time of purchase. See if you can get the speaker to provide you with a stack of business cards if their complete contact information is not on the customer's copy of their order form.

This way the customer can contact the speaker directly with any questions on product, fulfillment, returns, etc. This keeps this follow-up activity out of the promoter's hands and in the speakers where it should be.

TIP #56
Passing Out Promotional Materials

You should **NOT allow** event attendees to pass out any promotional materials, advertising specialties, event brochures, or other items to your attendees. At every event, there seems to be the one person who tries to place on every seat their brochure or sales flyer during the break.

You should have a member of your staff assigned to the task of making sure the tables and chairs remain "clean" between speakers. Anything in your room that is designed to attract the attendee's dollars can be taking them away from your back-of-the-room dollars.

I've seen stacks of flyers placed on tables near the sales table with the claim that it is a public area. I've seen boxes of shirts delivered to the event hotel to be passed out. I've even seen post-cards placed above every urinal in the men's room. All of these are a big no-no in the event industry.

TIP #57
Harvesting Names Revisited

We talked earlier about not letting your speakers harvest names from your crowd by offering freebies to try and capture attendee information for their database. In the previous tip, we talked about not allowing your attendees to pass out promotional materials to the audience. It's your crowd, and you're the one that spent your time and money to get them in the room.

This next tip is kind of a combination of the two — don't allow your attendees to harvest the names from your audience by passing around a notepad to have everyone write down their contact information. If this happens, you or a member of your staff needs to discretely locate this list and keep it. You want to do it without making a scene. Nobody will know what happened to the list, and few will ask about it.

How does this impact your bottom line? Anyone else marketing to your list has the possibility of pulling dollars away from you to themselves. It's your list — protect it.

TIP #58
Hey Big Spender

If you've done an event previously, you'll know who the big spenders at your event were. There is always at least one or two in every crowd — that guy or gal who seems to follow every speaker back to the sales table and orders their event package. They can easily spend $10,000, $15,000, $20,000 or more at your event.

So what do you need to do? Make sure you get them to your next event. How? By doing almost whatever it takes. Make them a VIP. Give them a special registration discount. Let them have a private breakfast with you. Just get them there.

Be sure to monitor your returns before deciding if someone deserves special consideration. It doesn't do much good to have someone purchase several packages but return 80% of them for refunds after the event.

TIP #59
Speaker Follow-up

Make sure your speakers understand they are expected to follow up promptly with anyone that purchased their package at your event with an appropriate thank you email or note. This should be separate from any acknowledgements that might come from you, the promoter.

If someone has just spent hundreds or thousands of dollars on a product then you definitely want to make sure the sale sticks. A note reiterating what a wise decision the buyer has made and restating what all they'll receive will go a long way towards your achieving that objective.

TIP #60
Prices Ending in "7"

I don't know why it is. For whatever reason, prices that end in the number "7" generate more sales than prices ending in other digits. This has been tested widely on the Internet and in other venues and has consistently proven to be true.

So why argue with the facts? Just request that your speakers make their product offers $497, $997, $1,997, $2,997 or any number ending with the digit "7". It'll put more money in both of your pockets over the long run.

TIP #61
Keep Them In The Vicinity

As your event unfolds, more of your speaker's products will begin to appear on your sales table. People may be pondering which continuing education offers they want to take advantage of before the event has concluded.

So you want them to be around the sales table reviewing speaker's materials as much as you can. You can keep them in the vicinity by setting up your coffee stations and break tables near your sales table. People will naturally be drawn to the area due to the refreshments and snacks being located nearby.

Your sales table is not the break table, though. Be sure there is a cart or separate space for people to place trash and dirty dishes.

Of course, you don't want to stack products right on top of each other, as you need ample room for people to order product, but anything you can do to keep bringing them back to the sales area is beneficial.

TIP #62
Batch Out Daily

his tip sounds like a no-brainer, but I've made the mistake of forgetting before. So I thought I'd pass it along. Remember to batch out your credit card terminal(s) at the end of the day if you're processing cards in real time at your event.

The wheels aren't set in motion for you to get your money from the merchant account provider unless you communicate all the day's transactions to them electronically by "batching" out your terminals. So don't forget this simple step.

TIP #63
Keep It Looking Professional

Make sure your sales table area looks professional throughout your event. Nothing screams "amateur" more loudly than a tacky looking and disorganized sales area.

Make sure all your tables are skirted and boxes and miscellaneous materials are stored out of sight. Don't leave soda cans and coffee cups scattered around your table. Make sure you have a trash can handy and use it.

Keep the product and literature displays organized neatly. Product displays, if used over the course of several events, will take a beating from repeated handling, packing, and shipping. So "retire" dog-eared manuals and cracked CD or DVD cases as soon as they look less than their best.

TIP #64
What's Eating You?

I **f you've ever been to a** trade show you have probably noticed that during lunch booth personnel will grab a plate of food and bring it back to their booth to eat. When you approach that booth and see someone balancing a plate on their lap and that their mouth is full, are you inclined to interrupt them to ask a question about their product or service? Probably not.

Your sales table shouldn't be a dining hall either. People won't ask questions about products if they feel they're interrupting someone's meal. So keep food out of your sales area. Make sure you have enough staff on hand to allow your sales staff to slip away one or two at a time to eat in a more fitting location.

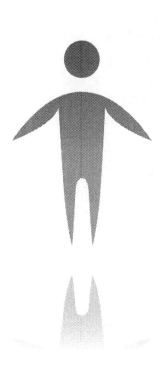

TIP #65
Don't Leave It Unguarded

Keep your order table manned at all times throughout the event. Don't leave speaker's products on display with no one responsible for keeping an eye on things. Despite your best efforts, sometimes a product will sprout wings and fly away without your knowledge. You just don't want to make it easy.

You'd think people who have spent a couple thousand dollars to attend an event would be honest, trustworthy people, and certainly almost all are. But I've had people crawl underneath a sales table after hours and steal product out of boxes that had been packed away.

While it's a bit of a pain to breakdown and setup a display table each day, it's something you've got to do. Public areas aren't very secure, and hopefully you'll have a room nearby that product and equipment can be locked up in safely overnight. If you don't, then you'll need to decide what items you need to take back to your sleeping room. Credit card terminals can cost upwards of $500 each, so we always make sure these are secured.

Not only do you want to make sure your table is manned at all times for security purposes, you also want someone to be available to answer questions about products.

TIP #66
Hotel Holding Fees

When planning how many of your own products you want to ship ahead of time to the hotel, keep in mind that larger properties typically charge a package receipt and holding fee for receiving your boxes. If you've decided you're going to deliver product to the attendees at the event rather than post-event, then just be aware ahead of time there are additional costs associated with this.

I've been hit with bills for $200 and more from some of the Las Vegas casinos for receipt of product and for shipping things back out after the event. Both of these can significantly eat into your back-of-the-room profits.

I'm not saying that you shouldn't send out product ahead of time. If that's your model, that's fine. Just know there are extra costs associated with this.

TIP #67
Hiding From Hurricanes

L et's face it — acts of God happen. Want to know a sure way to kill the back-of-the-room sales at your event? Simply have your event cancelled altogether due to a hurricane. I had to cancel hotel reservations and try to find out what the airlines were going to do on tickets when Hurricane Katrina pounded New Orleans.

What's this mean to you? Seriously consider avoiding the Gulf Coast and other hurricane prone spots during the peak hurricane season of June to September. It seems as if more storms every year are hitting the U.S., so why even take a chance? In the last year, two event promoters I personally know have had their events ravaged by hurricanes.

There are no guarantees wherever you have an event. An earthquake can hit Los Angeles anytime. A tornado can tear through the Midwest during the spring. A blizzard can hit Denver. But you're pretty crazy if you try to do an event in the South during hurricane season.

TIP #68
Don't Crowd Me

When planning your room layout, be sure to allow easy access to and ample room around your sales table for the attendees. I've worked events where they shoehorned the sales table into a back corner, and people had to squeeze between chairs to get to it.

Don't do it. Make sure people have plenty of room around your table. The claustrophobics in your crowd won't go near your sales table if they have to be packed in like a can of sardines.

TIP #69
Inside Or Out?

Should you set your sales table up inside the meeting room or in a public area just outside your meeting room doors? I've seen it done both ways, and both have worked just fine.

If you're planning to set up your sales table in a lobby area outside the meeting room, then you'll want to be sure to place it where people will have to flow by the table after they exit the meeting room.

The same holds true if you're planning on putting the sales table inside the meeting room. Place it where they must go directly past the table to exit the room. Do not place it on an opposite wall out of the way of the traffic flow. You want to be in the traffic flow.

If you're in the meeting room, you will want the sales table to be behind the crowd if possible so it's not a distraction from the speaker.

In general, the larger the crowd the more often I see the sales table placed outside of the meeting room. Since you tend to have more people ordering products, the ordering process can take slightly longer, and you don't want to be in the way of the next speaker's start time.

TIP #70
Cutting Their Teeth

If you're well-known as an event promoter, you'll have lots of would-be speakers approach you about speaking on your platform. They want to hone their skills and make their pitch from your stage because your audience is the target group they want to go after.

Don't let unproven speakers cut their teeth on your platform. You're not running a speaker training school! Until they've proven they can both deliver great content and close sales from the platform, don't you be their guinea pig.

Make them provide documented proof of their closing ratios from previous events they've spoken at. If they can't show you several successes, then stay away.

The same is true for proven speakers testing new offers from your stage. You'd prefer they go with the tried and true rather than testing with your audience, if at all possible.

TIP #71
Handout Hints

When handing out order forms** or other literature to your audience, make sure your people work their way from the back of the room to the front. If you begin in the front, all the eyes from the row you're working back will be watching the person passing out the handouts rather focusing in on the speaker's close.

Be sure you have staff people specifically assigned to the task of distributing order forms or other handouts as needed by each individual speaker. Your speakers should know in advance who the contact person is for literature distribution at your event.

You want the amount of time it takes to pass things out as short as possible, so have enough people assigned to this task to keep things moving. You can count the number of people seated in each row and count out the handouts before they are to be distributed. Simply cross stack the number of pieces needed for each row and you can get all your literature passed out in less then a minute.

TIP #72
Make Sure They Have A Product

I 've been to several events over the years where, when asked what their offer would be, the speaker replied "Oh, I'm not selling anything." When I informed the promoter of this fact, they were taken aback, as they were totally unaware this was the case.

You should know up front what each of your speaker's offers is going to be. You should know their price point(s) and what the basic package consists of. Make sure they are selling something from the stage. If they aren't planning to sell, should they even be on your platform?

There certainly may be a situation where a non-selling speaker is okay. Maybe they are your keynoter, and you have them on your platform to draw more attendees into your event. But usually no selling means no money in your pocket, so make sure they have a product.

TIP #73
The Countdown Clock

Someone on your staff needs to be responsible for letting the speaker know how much time they have remaining in their presentation. I wouldn't use an actual clock that's counting down right in front of their eyes — I think that's too much of a distraction.

What's most common is hand written pages with the numbers "20," "10," "5," "2" and "Time's Up" written on them in big enough numbers or letters for your speaker to be able to see them clearly from stage. The time remaining page should be displayed by a staff person from the back of the room so none of the attendees are distracted. Make sure the speaker acknowledges the time left display with a subtle nod of the head.

Despite your best efforts, some speakers will run over their scheduled time, even though they've acknowledge the time countdown sheets as they were displayed. Some may even do it intentionally. You'll have to deal with it and adjust your schedule accordingly.

TIP #74
Close The Sale — Now!

When a speaker is making their offer to your audience, DO NOT let them do it by sending people to a special online order link. Your attendees will have a variety of offers made to them over the course of your event. The buying window opportunity for an individual speaker's products will be during those first few minutes after they've spoken.

You lose all control of the sale if you're asking the attendees to go online at a later time to order the speaker's product. You're depending upon the speaker to set up a special order link so you make sure you receive proper credit for any sales generated as a result of your event. If you're comfortable with that arrangement that's your call — but we don't recommend it.

TIP #75
Who's Your Go-To Person?

Who at your event has the authority to make some decisions and see that things are getting done? Any big decisions should obviously be yours as the event promoter, but it's up to you to decide what qualifies as a big or little decision.

But, more importantly, who can your attendees go to if they have any questions at all? Ideally, it is someone other than yourself, as you'll have your hands full making sure your event runs as smoothly as possible. So, designate someone on your staff to be the go to person, and make sure your attendees know that is who they can go to for assistance.

TIP #76
Lunchtime Losses

Invariably, you will lose some of the audience to lunch. Meaning, some people will be so hungry, they'll rush right by your order table to eat, therefore not ordering. Or, they'll be slow getting back from lunch and in a drowsy state.

The best way to control this is for you to be the lunch provider for the event. Allow your 15-minute order time after your last speaker completes his presentation before you even open up the lunch line.

On the back side, you can close your lunch line down when you want to start getting everyone headed back to the meeting room. When people see the crowds moving back to the meeting, they're pretty likely to follow along.

TIP #77
Speaker Preparation Room

Your speakers want to do as good of job as possible for you and for their own pocketbook. They are special, and they want to be treated as such, even if they don't say so. Give them a different style name badge then the regular attendees to make them stand out.

Also, give them a space of their own where they can prepare for their presentation. Arrange for a quiet room away from the crowd where your speaker can get his thoughts together to better deliver a home-run presentation for your audience. Have some bottled water and soft drinks available for them to wet their whistle.

You can also use this space to have them explain their offer(s) in more detail to your order taking team.

TIP #78
Burned Out Bulbs

Make sure a member of your staff has extra bulbs for any projection equipment on hand and knows how to quickly swap them out if you have a burn out in the middle of a speaker's presentation. Once you get a feel for bulb life, you may want to consider swapping in a fresh bulb at given intervals rather than waiting for one to burn out.

Anything that disrupts the flow of a speaker's presentation can disrupt your back-of-the-room sales.

TIP #79
A Consistent Look

Some of your biggest spending customers at the back of the room of your event will be people that have attended your events in the past. They're comfortable with you and have come to expect a certain look and feel for your events.

As you go from event to event, try to maintain a consistent look and feel for your events. Keep your order taking processes consistent, not only between events, but also from speaker to speaker within a single event.

Confusion only hampers sales. Help to avoid confusion by delivering what people expect from you.

TIP #80
Package Offers

I'm aware of some events where the promoter made a "Mega offer" that included products from several or all of the speakers. This package was offered at a discounted price versus purchasing the products individually.

This may or may not work for your event. It requires a large amount of communication and coordination with the participating speakers. Each speaker must be willing to accept less then they might have received per individual sale for being part of the package, but they may pick up more clients overall due to the package.

You'll have to decide if this is something worth testing at your event.

TIP #81
Bookstore Option

Some events feature a "bookstore" where other products are offered in addition to any of the speaker's packages. These are typically low-priced items like books or CDs that relate to the subject of your event.

The bookstore can be looked at from two viewpoints, and you'll have to decide if one is right for your event. Some people believe that any lower priced options you provide the attendees gives them an opportunity to spend a little rather than a lot on some of the higher-priced speaker packages.

Others believe that anything you can do to stimulate some buying behavior from your attendees is a positive thing, and it can raise some additional revenues for you at your event. I can see both sides of the coin.

From my history, I have not seen a bookstore in any way detract from the sales of a speaker. I've even had a product at an event for a speaker that was priced at a few hundred dollars go unsold while the several thousand dollar package that speaker offered at that same event sell very well.

But the work involved in setting up and running a bookstore at your event may not justify the return on investment. You'll have to decide what is right for you.

TIP #82
Keep That Extra Literature

As an event unfolds, you'll begin to accrue more and more literature from the speakers. Things like their handouts, their offer summaries, their order forms, etc. Be sure to keep these extras at the sales table, as you'll frequently have an attendee who comes in late or who missed a session for some reason and is interested in purchasing the package of the speaker they missed.

Any material you can have on hand that helps describe the offer and the material the speaker covered can help to close a product sale. There's no reason to dispose of any extra literature until after the event has concluded.

You'll want to keep a copy of all the literature distributed for your own records. A successful speaker's order form can be a great model for you to follow for your own product or service offerings at an event.

TIP #83
Friendly Competition

Sometimes your speakers will be fiercely competitive —
with each other. It's usually a friendly competition, although
I know of some speakers who truly dislike other speakers
sharing the same platform. In the "friendly competition" environ-
ment you'll have speakers who constantly want to know if they
were the "Top Dog." In other words, did they sell more then anyone
else at the event?

Of course you'll be sharing each speaker's results with them
individually. But it's really not any of their business what the
specific dollar sales were for each speaker at your event. If I'm
cornered by a speaker wanting to know specific results of other
speakers I won't give them an answer other than their own dollar
sales and whether they are the "Top Dog" or somewhere in the
middle of the pack in terms of results.

TIP #84
Continue to Educate Yourself

I **f you're a professional event promoter,** than you'll never want to stop learning more about your industry. New things are happening all the time, and you need to continue to educate yourself about event promotion tactics and strategies.

A group I've recently become involved with that I would encourage you to check out is the "Seminar Marketing Alliance Resource Team" (SMART). This group, founded by BigSeminar promoter Armand Morin and Debra Thompson of the Next Level Institute, teaches aspiring and existing event promoters the inside and outside information on how the seminar business really functions. As a special bonus for you, I've arranged for a free month's trial membership in SMART.

Simply go to SeminarMarketing.com/Bret and enter your name and email address for your temporary pass.

TIP #85
Manning the Microphone

If a speaker asks questions of the audience, you run the risk of having an attendee hijack your microphone and ramble on for several minutes. Obviously, this is not a desirable scenario for your event in most cases.

The best way to control the microphone is to have specially designated microphone runners who are responsible for moving to the person in the audience who wishes to talk. Then, have the microphone runners physically keep a hold of the microphone as the person is speaking. If they relinquish the microphone to the attendee, you have a far greater chance of losing control of things.

TIP #86
Disorganized Organization

his one sounds kind of funny, doesn't it? What I'm speaking of here concerns the arrangement of sales literature on your sales table. If the literature is something you want the attendees to pick up and take with them, you shouldn't have your stacks arranged in such pristine condition that the attendees are afraid to pick anything up for fear of messing up your sales table.

If you have flyers or order forms on the table, fan them out in a neat manner, but in a way that it's obvious to the attendees that they can take one with them if they want. So, be organized — but not too organized.

TIP #87
The Expanding Sales Table

As your event goes by, you will accumulate more literature from the speakers, as well as the speaker's products to display on your sales table. Make sure you have the space to add more sales tables as needed. You don't want for things to be so crammed together that it looks shoddy or so spread out that the table looks barren.

Know who your hotel contact is so you can quickly have an additional table added (or subtracted) during a break or at the end of the day. If your order table is set up inside your meeting room, never move things around during a speaker's presentation.

TIP #88
Can You View It From the Back?

If your meeting room is deep, you may have an issue with those people sitting in the back of the room being able to read the PowerPoint slides of a speaker. You should know well in advance of your event what your room dimensions are going to be.

You should communicate this information in advance to your speakers, along with a recommendation on font size for their PowerPoint slides so that the people sitting in the back can still read what's on the screen. It can be very disruptive to have the people in the back of the room continually asking for the speaker to repeat a URL or some other information from a slide because it's not big enough on the screen.

TIP #89
Photo Ops

A fter a speaker finishes their sales close, you will be leading them back to the sales table. If you have an event photographer, arrange to have them at the sales table at this same time.

When a customer invests in a speaker's product, have your photographer take a picture of that customer with the speaker and get it to the customer during or after the event. The speaker is a celebrity to most of your customers, and the opportunity to have their picture taken with the speaker can be a huge incentive to sign up for that speaker's package.

I recommend you check out the folks at SeminarPhotography.com if you need an event photographer.

TIP #90
The Back-of-the-Room Screen

I **was recently at an event where** I saw a new technique that I thought was pretty neat. In addition to the multiple screens they had across the front of the room, they also had a full-sized screen in the back of the room facing the stage.

This screen was used in two primary ways. First, the promoter used it as their "countdown clock" for the speakers, showing the speaker how much time they had remaining in their presentation.

Secondly, if the speaker was using a PowerPoint presentation it was also projected up on this screen. This allowed the speaker to keep facing forward to the audience rather than turning their back to read their own PowerPoint slides off the screen behind them.

The more your speaker can maintain eye contact with your audience, the better rapport they'll establish and the better the back of your room sales should be.

TIP #91
The Range of Your Clicker

If your speaker is using a remote clicker to change their Power Point slides, be sure you know the range of the clicker, as well as the specific direction the clicker must be pointed.

At a recent event with over 500 people, the speakers had continual problems with their PowerPoint presentations. The reason — the room was so large, the speakers couldn't aim their clicker accurately on a consistent basis.

So, be sure your room set-up allows for any PowerPoint presentation to function flawlessly.

TIP #92
Put It on a Pedestal

A **speaker's product is his or her** "baby." That speaker should treat it with tender loving care on the stage, as if it's of very high value and should be handled very carefully. So what's with that speaker who holds up part of his package to show your audience as he's doing his sales close, and then tosses it to the ground like it's not worth the paper it's printed on.

If they don't appear to value their product, then what's your audience going to think about their product? Probably not much. So be sure your speakers know that you have a table on the stage to display their product on and to place the product back on after the speaker has held it up for demonstration.

TIP #93
Best Months to Schedule Your Event

We talked earlier about avoiding the Southeast during hurricane season. But, in general, what are the best months to hold your seminars? According to seminar expert Fred Gleeck's book, *Marketing and Promoting Your Own Seminars and Workshops*, the research has already been done for you.

Here are the results:

Rank	When the Participant is Paying	When Someone Else is Paying
#1	January	March
#2	September	October
#3	October	April
#4	March	September
#5	April	November
#6	June	January
#7	November	February
#8	February	June
#9	May	May

#10	July	July
#11	December	August
#12	August	December

Obviously, the more people you can draw to your event, the better your chances of increasing your back-of-the-room sales.

TIP #94
Best Days of the Week to Hold Your Event

You also need to look at the best days of the week for holding your event. Also from Fred Gleeck's *Marketing and Promoting Your Own Seminars and Workshops* comes the following information:

Rank	When the Participant is Paying	When Someone Else is Paying
#1	Saturday	Wednesday
#2	Sunday	Thursday
#3	Thursday	Tuesday
#4	Wednesday	Friday
#5	Tuesday	Saturday
#6	Friday	Monday
#7	Monday	Sunday

TIP #95
Wet Their Whistle

Keep some bottled water or other suitable refreshment on stage for your speakers to be able to wet their whistle with as needed during their presentation. A scratchy voiced speaker is less likely to "connect" with your audience.

So, take the time to make sure the speaker has what he or she needs on stage before they begin talking. Then, they won't have to interrupt the presentation to request some water.

TIP #96
Pre-Event Speaker Meeting

In order to help your event flow as smoothly as possible, you should have a speaker meeting the evening before your event is scheduled to begin. Make sure each speaker understands the following:

→ When they speak

→ How much time they have

→ How they will be informed of time remaining during their presentation

→ What to do with any handouts or order forms they want passed out

→ To communicate with the event audio/video people about any special requirements they may have

→ Where they are to go upon the conclusion of their talk

➜   The need to communicate to the sales staff
        what their offer is going to be

Simply put, try to avoid any surprises for your speakers or your staff. Make sure you find out who the speaker intends to have available as your contact person within their organization for post-event questions.

TIP #97
Mega Events

If you're going to have an event with more than 500 participants, you will need to reassess some of your sales processes to make sure your sales area can handle any table rushes or the general overall anticipated increase in sales. Some of the factors you'll need to be aware of include:

→ Is your merchant account capable of handling the larger dollar volumes? I've seen events reach seven figures in sales, and if your merchant account isn't set up for this kind of volume, you could run into problems. There's nothing worse than a merchant account provider freezing funds for six months because you hadn't communicated with them the amount you expected to process at your event.

→ Take a look at where you want to set up your sales table(s). Look at where your traffic will be exiting the meeting room. You may want more than one order station to ease the ordering process.

193

→ Make sure you have generic order forms available because some of your speakers will invariably under produce the number needed

→ Look at the length of your breaks and lunches. It will take longer to move people in and out of the room, so be sure you allow sufficient ordering time

TIP #98
Order Form No-Nos

I f your speakers are providing their own order forms, be sure that their order form is customized to your event or, at the least, is generic and doesn't specifically reference a previous event that the speaker made a presentation at.

Your audience wants to feel special, and if you or any of your speakers are using retread handouts or order forms, then both your speaker and you aren't usually viewed in a favorable light.

TIP #99
Should You Accept Checks?

In a word — Yes! In the dozens of events our company has handled the back of the room sales for, I've only had one customer write a bad check at an event.

Although the majority of your attendees will pay with credit card, you will have some that don't use credit cards and want to make purchases by check or even cash. Take their money. Just be sure to clearly notate on their order form if you've taken payment in any form other then credit card so you can keep track of your accounting properly.

TIP #100
Location Considerations

Where you hold your event can obviously have a significant effect on your back-of-the-room sales. The more people you can get there, the more money you will make. Therefore, when you're choosing the city to hold your event in, one of your primary criteria should be how easy it is for people to get there.

The major locations in which events are held include:

➔   Atlanta

➔   Los Angeles

➔   Orlando

➔   Phoenix

➔   Dallas

Other major cities readily accessible via air include Seattle, Portland, Kansas City, Chicago, Miami, San Francisco, Denver, Washington, New York and Boston. If you're just starting out you're best to stick with the major cities if you want to draw a larger crowd.

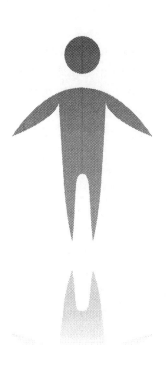

TIP #101
Speak at Your Own Event

If you're an expert on a subject that relates in any way to the primary focus of your event, then you should definitely speak on your own platform. Not only does it give you an additional opportunity to build rapport and trust with your audience, aside from any emceeing duties you may perform, it also provides you the opportunity to sell your own products and/or services from the platform.

Any sales you generate are not subject to the normal 50/50 promoter/speaker split because you're both the promoter and the speaker. Ah, ain't life grand!

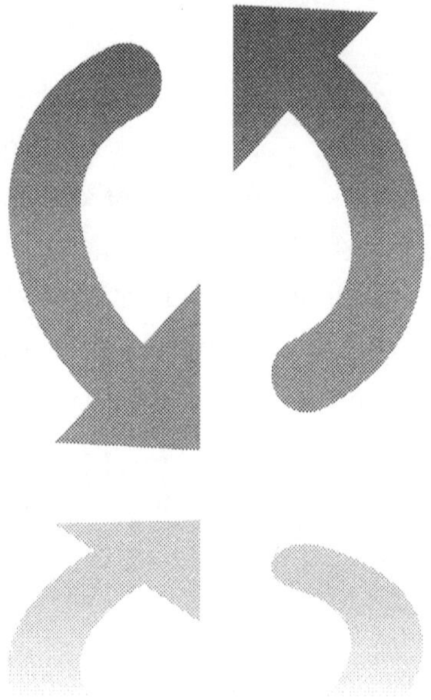

BONUS TIP #1
SFSBookstore.com

Interested in marketing, advertising, and copywriting? If you're promoting events you should be. Speaker Fulfillment Services has a special website that features dozens of the top books ever written on the subjects of:

→ marketing

→ advertising

→ copywriting

→ information marketing

→ consulting

→ seminar marketing

→ Internet marketing

→ and much more!

You'll find classics from the old masters like Claude Hopkins, John Caples, John E. Kennedy, E. Haldeman-Julius, and Clyde Bedell, as well as newer titles from pros like Dr. Jeffrey Lant, Fred Gleeck, Carl Galletti and others.

Just visit SFSBookstore.com for a complete listing of the titles available. Here's some of what you'll find:

→ *1001 Ways to Market Your Books* — John Kremer

→ *Breakthrough Advertising* — Eugene Schwartz

→ *The First Hundred Million* — E. Haldeman-Julius

→ *How To Make $20,000.00 An Hour Without A Gun For Professional Speakers and People Seriously Interested in the Business of Speaking* — Dan Kennedy

→ *How to Make a Whole Lot More Than $1,000,000 Writing, Commissioning, Publishing and Selling "How-To" Information* — Jeffrey Lant

→ *How to Write Advertising That Sells* — Clyde Bedell

→ *How to Write a Good Advertisement — A Short Course in Copywriting* — Vic Schwab

→ *Marketing With Postcards* — Alex Mandossian

→ *My Life in Advertising/Scientific Advertising* — Claude Hopkins

→ *Ogilvy on Advertising* — David Ogilvy

→ *Reason Why Advertising plus Intensive Advertising* — John E. Kennedy

→ *The Robert Collier Letter Book* — Robert Collier

→ *Tested Advertising Methods* — John Caples

BONUS TIP #2
Get SMART

Top **event promoters like** Armand Morin, Debra Thompson, Heather Seitz, and Robin Thompson have banded together to form the Seminar Marketing Alliance Resource Team (SMART). If you're new to the event promotion scene or a seasoned veteran who wants to learn some of the nuances of putting on your events than you should check out SMART. Go to <u>SeminarMarketing.com</u>.

SMART offers a comprehensive training program that will teach you all the ins and outs of putting on your own events. You'll learn about:

→ How to avoid getting taken by hotels

→ How to handle your speakers

→ How to put cheeks in your seats

→ Resources SMART promoters use

→ And much, much more

BONUS TIP #3
Some Freebies for You

Fred Gleeck offers several of his books in digital format for no charge. They contain some excellent information for speakers and event promoters and are well worth downloading and printing out for your own use.

The following titles are available:

→   *Marketing and Promoting Your Own Seminars and Workshops*

→   *Publishing for Maximum Profit*

→   *Selling Information: How You Can Create, Market and Sell Knowledge in Any Field*

→   *Speaking for Millions: How to Make Really Big Money as a Professional Speaker*

→   *Selling Products from the Platform*

To get your FREE copies of these books go to:
<u>FredGleeck.com/ebooks</u>

BONUS TIP #4
Additional Speaking Related Resources on the Internet

→ Simply Speaking Ezine by Lenny Laskowski — LJLSeminars.com

→ Great Speaking Ezine by Tom Antion. Site also has lots of great articles for speakers and meeting planners

→ SpeakerMatch — The fastest and easiest way to locate the perfect speaker for your next event

→ Toastmasters International, Toastmasters.com. A great way to improve your communication skills and lose your fears of public speaking

→ National Speakers Association — NSASpeaker.org

→ GettingPaidToSpeak.com by Mary McKay — Discover how to secure paid speaking engagements by systematizing the booking process.

→ Professional Convention Management Association — PCMA.org

→ Meeting Planners International — MPIWeb.org

→ Seminar Marketing Alliance Resource Team (SMART) — SeminarMarketing.com

→ Speaker Training Summit — LesSpeaks.com

→ John Childers' Million Dollar Speaking Training — JohnChilders.com

For the complete current list visit SFSRecommends.com

About Speaker Fulfillment Services

Speaker Fulfillment Services provides services for both event promoters and for speakers, authors, and other information marketers.

First, for selected clients, Speaker Fulfillment Services can provide back-of-the-room, order-taking services at your event. If you don't have a merchant account or if your merchant account is not classified correctly or set up to handle a large volume of business in a short period of time, SFS can help.

We provide the staff to handle your back-of-the-room sales and take care of all the processing, communicating of order information to your speakers, provide you with a sales breakdown by speaker, and take care of paying your speakers and yourself after the event.

The second major service SFS provides is duplication and fulfillment of information products. We can duplicate your CDs or DVDs, print your manuals, and assemble your packages in ready-to-ship-to-your-end-customer condition. Discs can be thermal printed or have paper labels applied and manuals can be done in three-ring binder, spiral bound, comb bound or saddle stitched formats.

You can also warehouse your information products with SFS that have been produced elsewhere, such as books, and we will ship out your orders for you.

213

For more information on any of these services contact
Speaker Fulfillment Services at 812-235-8050
or email <u>Info@SFSMail.com</u>

About Bret Ridgway

Bret **Ridgway is the founder of** Speaker Fulfillment Services, a company that provides event promoters with back-of-the-room order processing services and information marketers with product duplication and fulfillment services. Bret has been coordinating back-of-the-room sales activities for events since 1999 with his partner Bryan Hane.

Bret is a frequent guest speaker on teleseminars where he talks about the subject of product creation and packaging strategies. He has developed numerous information products of his own in conjunction with Internet marketing and information marketing experts such as Alex Mandossian, Armand Morin, Fred Gleeck and others.

He has also developed numerous websites including the class marketing book site SFSBookstore.com and the leading industrial maintenance portal and catalog site at MaintenanceResources.com.

Bret resides in Terre Haute, Indiana with his wife of 21 years, Karen, and his three children — Christina, 18, Jacob, 16, and Mitchell, 13, along with their 2 dogs, 5 cats, and 1 guinea pig.